BEASTGIRL
&
Other Origin Myths

ELIZABETH ACEVEDO

Sarah —

handwritten inscription and signatures

BEASTGIRL

& Other Origin Myths

FIRST EDITION, 2016
THIRD PRINTING, 2017
ISBN 978-1-936919-45-1
PRINTED IN THE UNITED STATES OF AMERICA

PUBLISHED BY YESYES BOOKS
1614 NE ALBERTA ST
PORTLAND, OR 97211
YESYESBOOKS.COM

KMA SULLIVAN, PUBLISHER
JILL KOLONGOWSKI, MANAGING EDITOR
STEVIE EDWARDS, SENIOR EDITOR, BOOK DEVELOPMENT
ALBAN FISCHER, GRAPHIC DESIGNER
BEYZA OZER, DEPUTY DIRECTOR OF SOCIAL MEDIA
AMBER RAMBHAROSE, CREATIVE DIRECTOR OF SOCIAL MEDIA
PHILLIP B. WILLIAMS, COEDITOR IN CHIEF, *VINYL*
MARK DERKS, FICTION EDITOR, *VINYL*
JOANN BALINGIT, ASSISTANT EDITOR
MARY CATHERINE CURLEY, ASSISTANT EDITOR
JOHNNA C. GURGEL, ASSISTANT EDITOR, PUBLICITY
COLE HILDEBRAND, ASSISTANT EDITOR
CARLY SCHWEPPE, ASSISTANT EDITOR, *VINYL*
HARI ZIYAD, ASSISTANT EDITOR, *VINYL*

FOR MAMI

who taught me to love storytelling

CONTENTS

LA CIGUAPA

For the Antilles

They say La Ciguapa was born on the peak of El Pico Duarte.
Balled up for centuries beneath the rocks
she sprang out red, covered in boils, dried off black
and the first thing she smelled was her burning hair.

* * *

They say Atabeyra carried La Ciguapa while in frog form—
held her low in the belly until squatting she laid her
into soft dirt: an egg made of ocean. Millenniums later, La Ciguapa
poked through and the blue water burst, grafted onto her skin.

* * *

They say La Ciguapa pried apart her jaw
and spit herself out, soft and malleable
but at the last second her legs scraped against fangs
and inverted her footing.

* * *

Her backwards-facing feet were no mistake, they say,
she was never meant to be found, followed—
an unseeable creature of crane legs, saltwater crocodile scales,
long beak of a parrot no music sings forth from.

* * *

La Ciguapa, they say, was made on one of those ships; stitched
and bewitched from moans and crashing waves. She emerged
entirely formed. Dark and howling, stepped onto the auction
block but none would buy her. They wouldn't even look her in the eye.

* * *

They say she came beneath the Spanish saddle of the first mare.
Rubbed together from leather and dark mane. Hungry.
That she has a hoof between her thighs and loves men
like the pestle loves the mortar;

                    she hums them into the cotton thick fog
of the mountains. They follow her none word sing-song
and try to climb her, tall and dark and rough as sugarcane
and don't know until they're whittled down how they've scraped

themselves dead. They say the men were the first to undo her name;
thinking that burying it would rot her magic, that long cry
they were compelled to answer. They hung all five-toed dogs
because they alone knew her scent—

they say there was a time her silhouette shadowed the full moon.
                                * * *

They say. They say. They say. Tuh, I'm lying. No one says. Who tells
her story anymore? She has no mother, La Ciguapa, and no children,
certainly not her people's tongues. We who have forgotten all our sacred
                             monsters.

BROTHER MYTH

A chub cheeked one. One of hollow face.

The milk brother is tall, bull-chested,
the shine of his father.

The other is boiling marmalade,
quivering stomach, quick bite.

It's okay to think of Cain and Abel.

Like them, one of these two
also heard voices. Was considered unwell.

The younger brother is the yucca's bark.
Earth-dark. Coarse. Having become only skin.

The older brother is the flesh.
Where the goodness pulses. Where hunger's quelled.

The sister? Like all sisters, the storyteller.

One brother, difficult to tell which from a distance,
leads the other to a field on fire.

There these men dance beneath an awning.
Knitted shadows of brothers past.

The knife, when a brother reveals it, a thing of magic,
a thing of awe. They both marvel at the first sparkle of blood.

Neither cries. Neither cries out.
There is no tussle as one learns what must happen.

He casts out his arms. He waits. When the carving is done
he wears his grotesque skin like a fine new robe

and they are known for what they have truly been.

CONVERSATIONS

My mother calls and sandbag sighs
into another of her lists:

She found Papi shivering inside
a bottle of spiced rum. Again.
My grandparents' bills won't origami
into pretty swans. My brother
doesn't drink the milk anymore—
he knows about the medicine.

There is a timer on these calls
but the bread always burns in her irises.
I put the match out on her throat.
When I was little, she never cried
where I could see her;
hung rosaries from her eyelashes instead.

I convinced myself silence was strength.
Won't feed from her fingers
the hardened aches she offers.
I fold into two walls, hide from her hands.
Peel my ear when she reminds me
daughters are meant to veil themselves behind the skirt
of their mothers. *When are you going to visit?*
I don't tell her this is why I left.

You know, I know . . . it's easier to be far from this. From me.
We both heave   wordless.
She whistles softly through her teeth
and I am packed with the air of her.

S A L T

After Pariah *by Marcos Dimas, c 1972*

A carton of salt had been placed on the rocky ledge separating me
from the Hudson River. I climb, grab, pour a dime
into my palm. Didn't know then it was left as an offering.
Mami upends the back of my hand. Says, *Deja eso, eso lo dejó una bruja.*

For a whole month I'm afraid to sleep. Clutch my Barbie sheets
afraid my seasoned hand will float and claw at air on its own.
Afraid there is someone other than me in this body. Mujer embrujadora,
you of all things knotted and kinked, skin of every color found in plum,
of storm torrents, of flesh that knows the collision between cuerpo
and malecón:

Mami sensed the salt inside, knew the blue dog you are painted to be.
Close-lipped witch, I've felt your cowrie shells of teeth along my wrists.
I've learned to chew magic like it was cassava. Woke one morning

carrying a red sun for a forehead. You taught me that—how to cross my ankles
but sharpen my daggers, how to hoist myself at the water's edge,
how to pose pretty then file my nails into stones, twirl
in circles of rum-scented cigar smoke. Here, now, alone.

PRESSING

The living room is haloed Mary, wooden crosses, psalms
the glass-wrapped candles: tall, thick
burn, mingle with incense   *Alleluia*

I sit on the sofa with the neighbors' girls
adorned in flouncy Sunday dresses & piety
this day is reserved for prayer circles & the women

thumb rosary ropes through calloused fingers
the neighbors' girls bow their heads, murmur underneath their breath
blessed are you . . . the fruit

I close my eyes & hold a couch cushion on top of my lap
press thumb to self fervently, moan along
is this prayer

When the circle comes to a close, Mami pulls me to her,
catches a whiff of my hand—*Jesus, did you bathe today, girl? Go wash, girl*
& I know this is a hidden thing, wash away thing, pray it out thing

Nightly, when everyone in my house is asleep, watch me roll onto belly,
my fingers find me unbidden, with bitten tongue
       I train myself quiet

I have a knowing about this unstopped need   does God watch
stop, slow down, speed up, circle, press & pray, & press & pray,
     press & suppress & pray   blessed are you

STRANGER TELLS ME
MY BODY BE A TEMPLE

and so I show him where
      I have stuck my fingernails
            beneath this chipping paint

spat on the stained glass
      used crooked backbone as scaffolding
            knowing it won't hold up a broken ceiling.

I tell him, *I've glugged down*
      the church wine and given sermon.
            Men flock but they never seem to come

for their spirits. If it were up to me
      I'd burn this altar nightly
            and dance alone in the rubble

pray that shitty pick-up line elsewhere.
      Because if anything this body is the pure
            holy of instinct

like closing your eyes
      and guiding an earring
            into long ago pierced flesh.

FIRST JOB

I rise with the bread.
Sleepy-eyed and yawning
walk the four blocks,
clock in and clean the windows.
Forget to lock the door.
Put the day-old bagels
near the front of the display.
Sweep. Wash the counters.
Check the register.
Forgot to lock the door.
By the time I hear the welcome chime
the man already has his dick in a fist, stroking.
Miguel, baking scones in the back,
hears me scream.
Laughs as he runs the man off.
Why your hands shakin', girl?
I forgot to lock the door.
And so I mop. Greet customers.
Percolate coffee. Warm bread.
Smile.
Pretend the girl inside of me
isn't just a small roach
always waiting for a broom to fall.

IT ALMOST CURDLES
MY WOMB DRY

Imagine the boys.
They will help me carry grocery bags.
Then whistle. Whisper.
Crook fingers in my daughter's direction.
She will accept their invitation.
Chill behind paint-chipped staircase.
The cheap vodka will burn her throat.
But not how they will later.
They become more thrust than thought.
Watch them grab wrists and ankles.
She is now a rope they jump.
For the years that follow.
She will wake me with her bed puddled in piss.
I will scrub these hands raw.
Tremble at what they could not prevent.
I hold all the smiles of my daughter.
Tipped up to the milk of this promise:
she will not walk hunched.
Forced to turn herself into a corner.
Taught her body it is a place to huddle.
She will not smile polite as men make war on her.
She will be carved from hard rock.
Sharpened   Shrapnel   A spearhead
Her whole body ready to fling itself
and arrow the hand of the first man
who tries to cover her mouth.

THE TRUE STORY OF LA NEGRA, A BIO-MYTH

La Negra is a beastgirl. From forehead to heel callused. Risen on an island made of shit bricks, an empire. The doctor pulled La Negra from her mother's throat: a swallowed sword, a string of rosary beads. La Negra's father is a dulled sugarcane machete. Crowned in her sun-dried umbilical cord, La Negra claws and wails, craves only mamajuana.

This is where she will end: enveloped in candlewax. Scratched & caught beneath your nails.

MAMI CAME TO THIS COUNTRY AS A NANNY

and around the same time she tells me i can't walk
the house wearing only panties anymore,
she teaches me how to hand wash them in the sink.
*tsk*ing that washing machines
don't launder as well as a good knuckling,
she drops soap on the crotch, folds the fabric
on itself and shows me how one end
pulls out the stains of the other—
detergent and fabric and hands against hands
make the seemingly most dirty material clean again.
no menstrual cycle ever made me more woman
in mami's eyes than this learning how to wash my own ass,
this turning of the shower rod into a garland of intimates—
this memory tightens my fist that first week of freshman year
when katie kerr's mother, who has a throat made for real pearls,
points her unsoftened mouth at me,
you better take care of katie, she's always had help.
and i have to blink, and blink, and blink but leave unmentioned
all the ways my hands have learned to care for things like her.

LIMINALITIES

Knuckles dug into the back of Janie's head. Fingernails scoured down her made-up cheek: a brillo pad cleaning pale china—did she scream?

—I can't remember, but still feel the rush of our pre-teen bodies rushing down the hill to watch. The thrill of being, for once, on the inside.

Blood from Janie's bottom lip stained her velour— this was back when the wanna-be-down white girls wore sweatsuits—but none of us stepped in, because even then we knew initiations required witnesses.

And although none of us liked Janie—the blue and blond of her, the Dominican guys she dated as she practiced speaking like us, the slang-faucet mouth she turned off when her mother was around—she probably shouldn't have been stomped out.

And I can't remember—really, I can't—why she was chosen.

If those of us that lived on this side of Amsterdam Ave. sat around the Little Park one day, and some older gang members asked if there was a girl at school that *could get dropped* and my schoolmates blanked and although I wasn't a part of this crew, only a neighborhood girl, friendly, wanting to be liked but afraid of bruising my own knuckles, if Janie's name, that I'd heard uttered since kindergarten, hardened in my mouth: an egg tumbling out firm and fat into the air

   a sacrifice, wasn't it, that fed some unknown god?

B E L O V E D

For Jordan Davis

it's easy to forget a pot of beans when you're numb.
the burning crinkled my nose but i didn't stir,
so when you come home

after work asking, *did you hear the verdict?*
i can only tell you i forgot to lower the heat,
that the stovetop stained where the beans split open

and pushed out from their skins; the boiling pot
sputtering blue-black water i can't bring myself
to clean.

cubans call this meal moros y cristianos,
the black beans and white rice cooked harmoniously.
today I'm convinced the cuban who named it that was being overly optimistic.

we say a silent grace over plain white rice.
and i wonder if you, like me, pray for an unborn child
we've already imagined shot in the chest.

tonight, no music plays and for the first time since i
learned to cook i understand
a meal can be a eulogy of mouthfuls.

neither one of us scrubs the stove. some things
deserve to be smudged. ungleaming. remembered.

P A R E J A

is the Spanish
word for pair.

Often used
to describe a romantic partner.

As in, *¿Dónde está*
tu pareja?

But pairing feels
like a heavy thing,

popped out of a mold
and perfectly aligned.

Do we match? I ask him.
Do we match?

And he shakes
his head no.

We're socks,
differently patterned

but holding tight
in the washer.

We are pant legs
patched at unmatched

points on the knees
but still creasing close.

We're more like gloves,
sometimes balled up

in separate pockets
but longing

not to lose the other.
This is what I imagine

he means, because my pair
ain't no poet,

so instead he says,
the best pairs aren't perfect

and so I translate
and know just what he means.

DOMINICAN SUPERSTITIONS

For sleeping: don't fall asleep with your knees up
or you'll invite a ghost to mount you.

For ghosts: never ask them what they want. That's
some American shit.

For ghosts that won't leave: use frankincense.
Conduct a rosary circle. Lead them to a tree that guards gold.

For nightmares: upon waking speak your dreams into the air—
the witnessing daylight will prevent them from coming true.

For nightmares in which teeth crumble like aged cassava:
someone you love has died. The teeth always know.

For menstrual periods: don't touch any child not your own
and don't wash your hair until you've bled for five days.

For the evil eye: cross yourself and stay away from folks
who would give a compliment but do not follow it with a blessing.

For reading: don't do it while eating.
For eating: don't do it while reading.

For kitchens: open an oven or open a refrigerator
but heat and cold air should never tangle in the same body.

For men: feed them well and feed them often—
the fatter the man the more likely he's too heavy to leave.

For cheating: watch out if you skip a hoop while fastening your belt
because one time too many means someone else has been minding your man.

For superstitions: treat them like salt, scatter them before you leave
and let them impale themselves into the soles of your feet.

THE DICTATOR'S BRUJAS *OR* WHY I DIDN'T GROW UP WITH DISNEY

I took her stories as first hand
when Mami told me how brujas
were the Dictator's favorite spies.

How he, Trujillo, would command they squat—
she imitated their sitting with one hand cupped in the other—
stooped like fat crows, their ears pressed to the zinc rooftops,
their one magic eye able to see through metal and minerals
and account for the rebels in the salons below.

Insurgency or simple insult resulted in the same—
being disappeared. And in that same cupped hand
Mami held me too. Imagining an island
where there was such a thing as magical espionage.
This shit was not Manhattan, and no Cinderella brujeria.

After Mami thought I was asleep, I wondered about the brujas;
what did they do when Trujillo was assassinated?
Did they yellow and wilt like plantain leaves?
Was their work for him merely forced labor and now free
they could go back to making jengibre balms
and setting bones and lighting fat candles for our dead?
Was the bad press too much? Crows shot in the hundreds
for being imagined witch-like? Did the brujas go underground,
take on normal jobs selling boletos and eggs

at the local colmado, and braiding hair
on the tourist beaches? Did they return to their families,
apply for visas, or climb onto a seaweed-covered yola
embarking for a city of honey where they could forget

the winged words that once drifted up to their ears,
that made them heavy and rush-filled with blood?

REGULARIZATION PLAN FOR FOREIGNERS, 1922

Trujillo says: *I will fix this.*
             And so the man digs the ditches.
The dirt packs beneath his nails and when his wife kisses
his fingers at night she tells him they smell of graves.

He holds her close, his bella negra of accented Spanish,
who does not think how a single word pronounced wilted
             could force him to dig a ditch for her.

Some nights, he dreams of yellowed eyes. Of sweat-drenched
dark brows. Bodies stacked like bricks
             building a wall that slices through the sky.

Borders are not as messy as people think.

They are clear, marked by ditches, by people face down,
head-to-ankle skin-linked fences: Do Not Cross.

Puedes ser nada disfrazado en piel y pelo?

He's learned to turn his ears down like a donkey
when the children of Haitians plead, *Yo soy Dominicano.*

At best they're mules,

             El Jefe tells the ditch digger, who is glad
he was born on this side of the flag. *This remedy will continue,*

El Jefe says. And so the ditch digger repeats the instructions
          like a refrain for cutting cane:

aim low, strike wide, look away as the open earth swallows them.

FEBRUARY 10TH, 2015

for a man nicknamed Tulile in Santiago, Dominican Republic

it never begins when the body hangs from a silk tree.

it always begins when the body hangs heavy and knotted
to the silk tree, and the tongue slips out of the mouth
—like a swollen maggot?—no, simply like a tongue.

this began when the body hung heavy from rope,
knotted to the silk tree and the tongue, swollen with creole,
slipped out of the mouth, a simple tongue.

it didn't begin with the tongue, swollen with creole,
slipping out between blue lips; hands bound as if praying
couldn't push the tongue back into the mouth.

did it begin with the tongue, swollen with creole,
the shoeshine polish on the long fingers clutching a winning
lotto ticket, a stolen lamp, the tongue bragging with glee?

it will begin again by forgetting the tongue, the black shoeshine polish
on the long fingers, winning or stealing, the dirt caked on bare feet,
the tree bowing low in the park plaza in this city of caballeros.

begin here: black polish, skin, dirt. a city named after gentlemen.
the shoeshine boy, not yet twenty, known by no real name,

known for no real reason, strung up the way only a black bruised body
   takes flight.

it never ends here—does it, ti cheri? The bodies hanging from silk trees.

JUAN DOLIO BEACH

The white man holds the girl's breast to the sunshine.
Rubs a thumb across the nylon fabric covering her nipple.
Squeezes. To test firmness? Ripeness. Her body
a highway-side fruit stand, she is chosen the same way
Momma taught me to pick avocados.

Don't stare, my cousin says. *It's just a part of the tourism.*
The girl bats at his hands, playfully. Not so playfully.
But I can't tell from here, where I toe the sand and sip *Presidente*.

The man's accent isn't English, the bills, Euros, wet
as he pulls them from his swim shorts' pocket.
She steps away. He pinches her ass. Playfully. Not so playfully.

I try to think of sex workers' rights as I watch her,
skin dark, thick patch of sun-lightened hair.
That age between twelve and unraveled womanhood.

The white man says something into her ear and laughs loud;
her smile is like the edge of a butter knife,
and my breath catches, can't tell if the sweat on my palm is mine
or the beer's. My throat becomes a tostonera

that presses the words flat

                    —Auxilio! Auxilio!—

the cries from a crowd near the water splits open the moment
and the girl runs toward the drowning.
The white man doesn't look at her as she runs
and neither do I.

LA SANTA MARIA

For Hispaniola

Leave that bitch at the bottom; wooden husk dulled and molded,
weighed with water. We don't need any more museums of white men.

Leave something for our black dead to play in. The bones of their once
brown bodies walking the Atlantic floor to dance around this first vessel.

We don't need his ship when he's already given us an ocean of ghosts—
imagine them in the thousands. Hundreds of thousands. Long released

from their skin crawling forward on an elbow, on a knee, knuckles, all gnaw.
Pressing eye-less skulls to the portholes. Knocking. Finally being let in to
  somewhere.

They stumble across the deck, touch the mottled curtains, spit on the iron
  fasteners,
place copper coins between the disks of their spine, dance.

I hope pirates have brushed fingers with these ghosts, that they've been led
to all the gold and pulled apart the ballast until it is nothing but a pile of
  splinters,

a great heap of wood meant to be left at the bottom; sell no tickets for this
  bringer
of apocalypses . . . but if, when you pull her up, you want to make a bonfire,

I've got the matches.

FOR THE POET WHO TOLD ME RATS AREN'T NOBLE ENOUGH CREATURES FOR A POEM

Because you are not the admired nightingale.
Because you are not the noble doe.
Because you are not the blackbird,
picturesque ermine, armadillo, or bat.
They've been written, and I don't know their song
the way I know your scuttling between walls.
The scent of your collapsed corpse bloating
beneath floorboards. Your frantic squeals
as you wrestle your own fur from glue traps.

Because in July of '97, you birthed a legion
on 109th, swarmed from behind dumpsters,
made our street infamous for something
other than crack. We nicknamed you "Cat-
killer," raced with you through open hydrants,
screeched like you when Siete blasted
aluminum bat into your brethren's skull—
the sound: slapped down dominoes. You reigned
that summer, Rat; knocked down the viejo's Heinekens,
your screech erupting with the cry of *Capicu!*
And even when they sent exterminators,
set flame to garbage, half dead, and on fire, you
pushed on.

Because you may be inelegant, simple,
a mammal bottom-feeder, always fucking famished,
little ugly thing that feasts on what crumbs fall
from the corner of our mouths, but you live
uncuddled, uncoddled, can't be bought at Petco
and fed to fat snakes because you're not the maze-rat
of labs: pale, pretty-eyed, trained.
You raise yourself sharp fanged, clawed, scarred,
patched dark—because of this alone they should
love you. So, when they tell you to crawl home
take your gutter, your dirt coat, your underbelly that
scrapes against street, concrete, squeak and filth this
page, Rat.

LA ÙLTIMA CACIQUE

Anacaona traveled music-like.
Leaving goosebump footprints on the spine
of the highest mountain.
She knew she'd have to hide,
when those men began to show
their skins did not clothe gods:

it was in their eyes. Blue and green as
Atabeyra's waters, but starved, clawing,
first the women, then the children,
the root vegetables from their beds.

They dropped gold
into the mouth of their hands
until her people had nothing more
than fisted wounds
for this never ending hunger.

Anacaona fled into the trees
where the earth thrusts at sky.
She should have fought,
it is easy to say.
But when they came
she merely tried to soothe them
like frothing dogs
that could not be patted to rest.

Who amongst us understands
a white man's anger?
They burned her people alive.
Gifted her a collar of rope,
cheered as her fingers scraped
at her throat for air.

It was a hot day. It always
is on the Island. Her toes made wind
as she swung, then grooves in the sand
as she was lowered and a world ended
and a new one cracked open:
swallowed us all.

ACKNOWLEDGEMENTS

I would like to thank the editors of the following print and online publications in which these poems, sometimes in different versions, appeared or are forthcoming:

Afro Latino Anthology: "Regularization Plan for Foreigners, 1922,"
    "Juan Dolio Beach" and "February 10th, 2015," Spring 2016
Crab Creek Review: "For the Poet Who Told Me Rats Aren't Noble Enough
    Creatures for a Poem," Fall 2016
Puerto De Sol: "Mami Came to this Country as a Nanny," "beloved" and
    "Regularization Plan for Foreigners, 1922," Fall 2015
Beltway Quarterly: "The Last Cacique," "February 10th, 2015" and
    "Dominican Superstitions," Fall 2015
Locked Horn Press: "La Santa Maria" and "La Ciguapa," Spring 2015
Notre Dame Review: "Conversations," Summer 2015
Poet Lore: "Salt," Spring 2015
Callaloo: "Pressing," Spring 2014
Madcap Review: "First Job," Winter 2015
The Ostrich Review: "Stranger Tells Me My Body Be Temple," Winter 2013

THANKS

Beastgirl & Other Origin Myths would not exist if it were not for so many amazing people who have supported me in doing this work.

Thank you first and foremost to my editor and publisher KMA Sullivan and the wonderful staff at YesYes Books for selecting this collection for publication and treating it with such care. Special thanks to Erin "Brooklyn Dolly" Robinson for allowing me to use her gorgeous artwork for the cover.

Thanks to all the amazing folks who read and edited *Beastgirl & Other Origin Myths*, often more than once, and helped me shape it into the best manuscript possible, including but not limited to: Clint Smith, Safia Elhillo, and Sarah Browning.

To my wonderful family: Papá y Mamá, my legion of cousins who answer my never-ending island questions, my aunts and uncles that love me like their own and keep the Christmas parties poppin', my older brothers Rob and Al who taught me how to beast from infancy, and special thanks to my parents who have supported my dream to tell our story.

To the many teachers and mentors in my life who encouraged me to keep writing, including: Phil Bildner, Abby Lublin, Silvia Canales, Josh Weiner, Jane Shore, Gregory Pardlo, Tony Lopez, H. Carrillo, my Brotherhood Sister-Sol family, and Urban Word.

To my students on the 2013-2016 DC Youth Slam Team and at Split This Rock for reminding me why this work matters.

Much love to the nurturing spaces that are CantoMundo, the Callaloo Writer's Workshop and Cave Canem.

To my fellow Beastgirls who never let me run alone: Carid, Cynthia, Kinshasa, Krystal, the Love Jones Girls and SLU.

To the Drawbridge Collective, I'm so glad we became friends. I can't imagine being an artist without having you all in my corner. I don't plan to ever find out.

Thank you to the islands that inspire me: Manhattan & Hispaniola. Pa'lante, siempre.

And lastly, I am most grateful to my beloved, Shakir Cannon-Moye. Thank you for co-writing the future with me. This love be no myth, and it lives here, always.

ELIZABETH ACEVEDO holds a BA in Performing Arts from The George Washington University and a MFA in Creative Writing from the University of Maryland. She is a National Poetry Slam Champion as well as a Cave Canem Fellow, CantoMundo Fellow, and participant of the Callaloo Writer's Workshop. Her work has been published or is forthcoming in the *Notre Dame Review*, *Callaloo*, *Puerto Del Sol*, *Poet Lore*, and *Beltway Quarterly*. Her manuscript, *Beastgirl & Other Origin Myths*, was a finalist for the YesYes Books Vinyl 45 Contest and released in October 2016, and her full-length collection, *Medusa Reads La Negra's Palm*, was the winner of the 2016 Berkshire Prize and will be published by Tupelo Press. She lives in Washington, D.C.

ALSO FROM YESYES BOOKS

FULL-LENGTH COLLECTIONS

i be, but i ain't by Aziza Barnes
The Feeder by Jennifer Jackson Berry
Love the Stranger by Jay Deshpande
Blues Triumphant by Jonterri Gadson
North of Order by Nicholas Gulig
Meet Me Here at Dawn by Sophie Klahr
I Don't Mind If You're Feeling Alone by Thomas Patrick Levy
If I Should Say I Have Hope by Lynn Melnick
some planet by jamie mortara
Boyishly by Tanya Olson
Pelican by Emily O'Neill
The Youngest Butcher in Illinois by Robert Ostrom
A New Language for Falling Out of Love by Meghan Privitello
I'm So Fine: A List of Famous Men & What I Had On by Khadijah Queen
American Barricade by Danniel Schoonebeek
The Anatomist by Taryn Schwilling
Gilt by Raena Shirali
Panic Attack, USA by Nate Slawson
[insert] boy by Danez Smith
Man vs Sky by Corey Zeller
The Bones of Us by J. Bradley
[Art by Adam Scott Mazer]